DIGGING FOR
DINOSAURS

Jessica Rose

Literacy Consultants
David Booth • Kathleen Corrigan

Contents

THE AGE OF THE REPTILES

Many scientists believe that millions of years ago, several kinds of dinosaurs roamed Earth. Dinosaurs came in many different sizes and had a wide variety of features. Some had bodies one-third of the length of a football field; others grew to a length of just three feet. Some dinosaurs had scales, others had feathers, and still others had both. Like animals today, dinosaurs did not all have the same eating habits: there were carnivores, herbivores, and scavengers too.

Based on evidence from fossils, many scientists believe that dinosaurs lived from 65.5 to 251 million years ago during the Mesozoic — or "middle life" — Era. Scientists study dinosaurs to better understand the world of today and its relationship to the world long ago.

The Mesozoic Era saw huge changes. It was a time of increasing diversity in the animal and plant worlds. This era is known as the Age of the Reptiles.

The *Alamosaurus* lived in southwestern United States during the Cretaceous Period.

A Geological Time Line

Evidence has led some scientists to believe that the geological history of Earth can be divided into a number of eras.

Cenozoic Era
(present–65.5 million years ago)

We are here

Mesozoic Era
(65.5–251.0 million years ago)

Cretaceous Period
(65.5–145.5 million years ago)
- The *Tyrannosaurus rex* rules the dinosaur world.
- Dinosaurs become extinct at the end of this period.

Jurassic Period
(145.5–199.6 million years ago)
- Large dinosaurs roam.
- The first birds appear.

Triassic Period
(199.6–251.0 million years ago)
- The first dinosaurs appear.
- Small mammals and flying and marine reptiles are already in existence.

Paleozoic Era
(251.0–542.0 million years ago)

Precambrian time
(542.0–4,600 million years ago)

5

WHAT ARE FOSSILS?

Scientists know so much about creatures that lived such a long time ago thanks to fossils. Fossils are the **preserved** remains of prehistoric plants and animals. They are links to living things of the past. There are many types of fossils, and they vary in size from huge leg bones to tiny shells.

Types of Fossils

There are two main types of fossils: body fossils and trace fossils. Body fossils come from the remains of animals. They include fossils of shells, bones, teeth, hair, and skin. Body fossils can tell us about what dinosaurs looked like.

On the other hand, trace fossils show evidence of dinosaur activity. They include fossils of footprints and burrows. These types of fossils can tell us what dinosaurs did. Not every organism will become a fossil. Fossils form only under specific conditions.

Trilobite fossils are very common. They have been discovered on every continent.

Mold and Cast

Mold and cast fossils are formed when an animal or plant quickly becomes covered with **sediment** after death. The sediment hardens around the dead organism, forming a mold. When the dead organism breaks down, it leaves an empty space inside the mold. Next, water flows into the mold. Minerals in the water then form crystals. These crystals perfectly fill the mold. Because mold and cast fossils are **created** deep underground, they become visible only when the top layers of sediment break down.

Formation of Mold and Cast Fossils

An animal's skeleton settles on the ground.

The sediment surrounding the skeleton hardens.

The skeleton dissolves, and a mold is formed.

Minerals form crystals inside the mold, and a cast is created.

The fossil is exposed on the surface of the earth.

Petrification

In some cases the tiny holes in the bones of a dead organism become filled with minerals from the surrounding sediment. Over time, minerals replace the bone material. When all of the bone material is replaced with minerals, the remains are turned into stone, or petrified. Petrified fossils are very common. When material is petrified, all the details

Petrified fossils are very detailed. Here, all the little bones in the feet and tail are clearly visible.

are preserved. A petrified bone will look like a natural bone, but it will be heavier and a different color.

Preservation

Sometimes an entire organism or part of an organism is preserved. Some animals may even become trapped in amber (tree resin) or ice. Both amber and ice perfectly preserve the organism. Such fully preserved **specimens** are very rare.

Common insects, such as this gnat, are often found in amber.

Impression

Some fossils are impressions of plants or animals. An impression is left when something presses into a softer material. For example, animals often leave tracks in the mud around rivers. Impressions form when the mud hardens and becomes rock. Impressions of footprints are very common. This makes sense because each dinosaur would have left many footprints but only one body. Impressions are a common type of trace fossil.

This is a dinosaur footprint impression in a rock found in Dinosaur Valley State Park, Texas.

Did You Know?

Amber is a fossil. Amber forms when tree resin fossilizes. Scientists believe that this process takes millions of years.

Resin drops on a tree

How Do We Find Fossils?

To find fossils, scientists look for certain conditions. Because dinosaurs were land animals, scientists look for dinosaur fossils in areas that were not covered by water during the Mesozoic Era. They also look in areas that are not currently covered by plants because plants make fossils difficult to spot. Dinosaur fossils exist only in rocks dating to the Mesozoic Era. So scientists look for exposed surface rocks that date from this era.

Finding fossils isn't new. People living in early civilizations found fossils, but they didn't know what they were. Many thought they were the remains of mythical creatures such as dragons.

Did You Know?

In the United States many fossils have been discovered along a wide stretch of land between Montana and Texas.

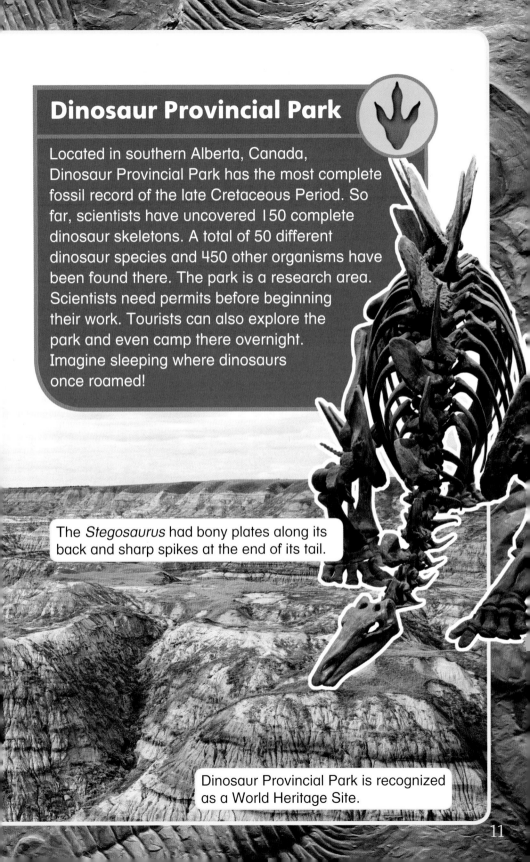

Dinosaur Provincial Park

Located in southern Alberta, Canada, Dinosaur Provincial Park has the most complete fossil record of the late Cretaceous Period. So far, scientists have uncovered 150 complete dinosaur skeletons. A total of 50 different dinosaur species and 450 other organisms have been found there. The park is a research area. Scientists need permits before beginning their work. Tourists can also explore the park and even camp there overnight. Imagine sleeping where dinosaurs once roamed!

The *Stegosaurus* had bony plates along its back and sharp spikes at the end of its tail.

Dinosaur Provincial Park is recognized as a World Heritage Site.

Fossils from a single dinosaur aren't always found together in one place. After a dinosaur died, other animals sometimes carried pieces of its body away. Many dinosaur bones may have been crushed under layers of sediment before they could become fossils. Even bones that have fossilized may resurface and be damaged or destroyed before somebody has a chance to discover them. As a result, dinosaur fossils are often scattered or incomplete. It's not uncommon to see just part of a dinosaur's skeleton in a museum.

Sue occupies a prominent spot in the Field Museum in Chicago.

Sue the *Tyrannosaurus rex*

Chicago's Field Museum is home to the largest, most complete, and best-preserved *Tyrannosaurus rex (T. rex)* in the world. The dinosaur is nicknamed Sue after Sue Hendrickson, the person who discovered it. Sue the *T. rex* is 40.5 feet long from snout to tail and 13 feet high at the hip. This dinosaur's fossils are so well preserved that scientists can even see where the muscles had been attached to the bones. While we don't know if Sue was male or female, we do know that it lived to be about 28 years old — pretty old for a *T. rex*. Sue was discovered in South Dakota, in the United States, in 1990.

Did You Know?

The first *T. rex* was discovered in 1902 by Barnum Brown. The name *Tyrannosaurus rex* means "tyrant lizard king."

WHO STUDIES DINOSAUR FOSSILS?

Just about anyone can go out and look for fossils. Some people stumble upon dinosaur bones completely by accident. Others dedicate their lives to searching for and studying fossils. These people are called paleontologists. Paleontologists are scientists who use fossils to study ancient life. Paleontology is a broad term that covers many different fields of study. Generally, paleontologists must understand both rocks and living organisms.

Field paleontologists are responsible for carefully excavating dinosaur fossils.

Meet a Paleontologist: Mary Anning

Mary Anning was born in 1799 in Lyme Regis, Dorset, England. Her family was not very wealthy. For fun, Anning's father took her and her brother for walks along the seashore. There they collected shells and fossils. Young Anning began selling what they collected to tourists. Around 1810 her brother discovered the first known *Ichthyosaurus* (pronounced ICK-thee-uh-sore-us), which Anning, not yet a teenager, carefully excavated. Anning herself was credited with several discoveries, including the first-ever *Plesiosaurus* (pronounced PLEE-see-oh-sore-us). Anning continued to collect specimens as an adult. Although she was not a trained scientist, she taught herself geology and paleontology by reading books and collecting samples. Anning became a well-respected figure among the mostly wealthy male paleontologists of the time. Many paleontologists traveled to Lyme Regis to study and buy her specimens.

Illustration of paleontologist Mary Anning with her collection of fossils

Did You Know?

The "she" in the widely known tongue twister "She Sells Seashells by the Seashore" is none other than Mary Anning.

In the field, paleontologists use a number of tools to dig for dinosaur fossils. Early paleontologists had simple tools such as chisels, hammers, and brushes. Many tools had other uses and were **adapted** for paleontological use. Today paleontologists have access to mapping and scanning equipment. These new technologies allow paleontologists to learn even more from the fossils they uncover.

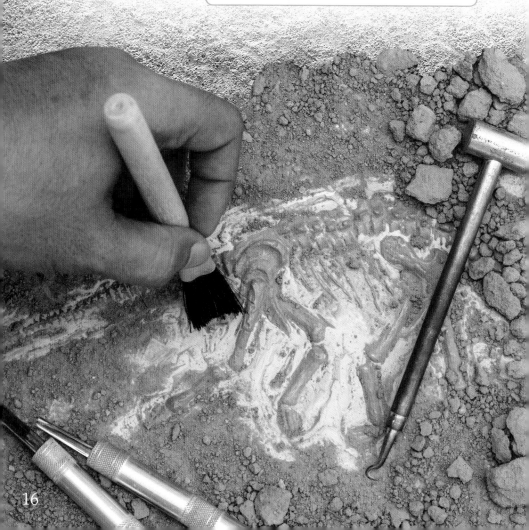

Special tools and lots of patience are often needed to extract a dinosaur fossil.

T. rex fossil

Excavating a Fossil

After a fossil has been found, paleontologists carefully remove the fossil from the ground. Fossils are excavated so that they can be studied in a lab. It is very important to make sure fossils are not damaged in the field. Paleontologists use a tried-and-true **method** to remove and **transport** fossils.

The first step is to clear the soil and remove the extra rock around the fossil. This way, the edges of the fossil can be clearly identified. It's important for paleontologists to figure out the size of the fossil in order to excavate the whole thing. For this purpose, paleontologists use tools such as rock hammers, chisels, picks, awls, and brushes.

Once the extra soil and rock around the fossil have been cleared away, paleontologists strengthen the fossil by applying an **adhesive** to its surface. Gauze, rice paper, or even toilet paper is applied over the adhesive. This protects the fossil from the plaster that is put on later.

Next, paleontologists dig a trench around the fossil. At this point, scientists wrap the top and sides of the fossil with strips of fabric soaked in plaster. Then the fossil is flipped, and the bottom is covered in the same way. This process is called jacketing. The jacket protects the fossil by keeping the sample rigid during transport.

In the laboratory the fossil is carefully freed. Then it can be cleaned and studied. Everything is carefully labeled, and every step is recorded.

Jacketed fossils can be very heavy. Sometimes helicopters are needed to transport excavated fossils.

A Paleontologist's Personal Field Kit

Paleontologists usually do fieldwork in remote areas. To be safe and successful in the field, paleontologists carry a reliable set of tools.

1. Paleontologists need to keep careful records. Note-taking equipment, such as hardcover, all-weather notebooks, pens, pencils, erasers, and rulers, is essential.

2. To protect themselves outdoors, paleontologists typically wear wide-brimmed hats, hiking boots, rain gear, and sunscreen.

3. Excavating in remote areas means that paleontologists often set up camp near their research site. Their camping equipment includes tents, sleeping bags, and headlamps.

4. Paleontologists need specialized tools, including a hand lens (to examine specimens in the field) and a rock hammer (to split rocks).

WHAT DO DINOSAUR FOSSILS TELL US?

Paleontologists have a lot to learn about fossils before the fossils end up on display or in storage. Fossils can reveal information about the dinosaur itself as well as the dinosaur's environment.

Dating Fossils

One of the most important things to learn about a fossil is its age. Knowing the age of a dinosaur fossil helps paleontologists understand when species appeared and when they died out. Scientists can't directly date the age of a fossil. The **radioactive** elements they need to examine in order to date ancient materials aren't found in fossils. However, these elements can be found in certain rocks. So paleontologists date the rocks found nearby in order to figure out the age of fossils.

Another way to know a fossil's age is by looking at how deeply it's buried. As time passes, layers of soil settle over the fossil and harden into rock. Older layers form on the bottom, and newer layers settle on top. If paleontologists know the date of one layer in a region, they can count backward to estimate the age of the buried fossil.

Putting Together Dinosaur Fossils

When you go to a museum, you may see displays of completely assembled dinosaur skeletons. These **reconstructions** allow us to see the magnificent sizes of these once-great beasts.

Psittacosaurus in Color

In 2016 a full-size, color reconstruction of a *Psittacosaurus* (pronounced sih-TACK-oh-sore-us) was revealed. The reconstruction is considered to be the most accurate model of a dinosaur ever made. The fossil of this *Psittacosaurus* is so well preserved that some of its color is visible to the naked eye.

By looking at the color pattern of the dinosaur, scientists determined that the *Psittacosaurus* was best camouflaged under a forest canopy. Sure enough, in the area where the dinosaur was discovered, scientists found evidence of evergreen trees.

Psittacosaurus reconstruction

Setting Up Sue

Sue, the *T. rex* from the Field Museum in Chicago, has more than 250 individual bones. By comparison, the human body has 206 bones.

Sue was removed after a 17-day excavation. In 1997 the Field Museum purchased the fossil for more than eight million dollars. To make sure that the fossil could be **analyzed** properly, the museum built a special laboratory for the project.

In this special laboratory, Sue's bones were carefully taken out of the rock. Workers used special tools to chip away at the rock while making sure not to damage the fossil. An important tool in fossil preparation is the air scribe. An air scribe is like a miniature jackhammer. Air scribes chip away at the hardened soil and rock around the fossil.

Air scribes come in a variety of sizes. The size used depends on how much material needs to be removed.

Sue's original fossils, except for the skull, are set up in the Field Museum. Sue's original skull is displayed on a balcony, where visitors can take in the massive skull from all angles. The museum also keeps copies, or casts, of Sue's bones for research purposes. Other complete copies travel around the world, allowing people from many different areas to see Sue in its entirety.

Did You Know?

It took more than 25,000 hours of painstaking labor to completely remove and clean every piece of Sue's skeleton.

Is It a Bird?

If you look at the foot of a *T. rex* and the claw of a bird, you'll find that they are quite similar. Scientists guessed that the mighty *T. rex* (and other dinosaurs) might be related to birds based on their skeletal structures. In 2008 a researcher at Harvard University found a protein in a *T. rex* fossil that showed that this dinosaur is related to birds.

Claw of a modern bird

Foot of *T.rex* Sue

Reconstruction: Not Required

In 2016 two small dinosaur wings were found trapped in amber in northern Myanmar, a country in Southeast Asia. Although these ancient wings are tiny, they are extremely detailed.

The specimens include bone, soft tissue, and feathers. The arrangement of feathers on the tiny wings is similar to the arrangement seen on birds today. For many in the scientific community, these wings confirm that the ancestors of modern birds were alive almost 100 million years ago.

This wing came from a small dinosaur no bigger than a sparrow.

Did You Know?

Also in 2016 the same team that found the wings found a feathered dinosaur tail in a piece of amber.

Looking Inside Dinosaur Eggs

Not only did dinosaurs have feathers like birds, but they also laid eggs like birds. The first dinosaur eggs were discovered in southern France in the mid-1850s. Back then, people believed that they were the eggs of gigantic birds.

For many years, looking inside a dinosaur egg meant destroying the fossil. The egg was either broken open, or the shell was dissolved using an acid. In the 1970s, a new type of medical scanner — CT — came into use. The CT scanner looks inside organisms without damaging them by taking many X-ray images from different angles. A computer then puts these images together to make an accurate reconstruction. A CT scan allows paleontologists to see what the inside of a dinosaur egg looks like without having to break the shell.

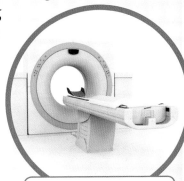

A medical CT scanner

According to Guinness World Records, the largest dinosaur egg collection, housed in the Heyuan Museum in China, totals 10,008 individual specimens.

Dinosaurs on the Move

Fossilized footprints can tell scientists a lot about dinosaurs. They reveal where certain types of dinosaurs lived and whether dinosaurs traveled alone or in groups. Scientists can also figure out a dinosaur's size by looking at its footprint.

Certain regions around the world have huge **concentrations** of dinosaur footprint and track fossils. One such area is Cal Orcko in Bolivia. Cal Orcko is home to about 5,000 dinosaur footprints from 462 individual trails.

Time and the movements of Earth can significantly change the landscape. Today these tracks make it look as though dinosaurs walked along the side of a steep cliff.

These tracks are preserved in a limestone rock that is roughly 4,000 feet by 350 feet in size. Visitors can look over this amazing rock face from a viewing platform, which is part of the museum at the site.

The rock face itself is always changing. Mining in the area, as well as natural erosion, continues to wear away at the exposed rock. Some fossils break away forever; others become uncovered.

Paleontologists often find large dinosaur footprints in the Gobi Desert. This footprint measures about 20 inches across.

Did You Know?

In 2016 a dinosaur footprint measuring 42 by 30 inches was found in the Gobi Desert, Mongolia. The footprint, likely belonging to a *Titanosaurus*, is one of the biggest dinosaur footprints ever found.

Dinosaur Diet

Have you ever wondered how we know what a dinosaur ate? There are many clues that help paleontologists answer that question.

Teeth

Dinosaur teeth are shaped differently depending on whether the dinosaur ate meat or plants. Dinosaurs that ate meat usually had larger teeth than dinosaurs that ate plants. For example, the *T. rex* had huge, jagged teeth that could latch onto prey. Some plant-eating dinosaurs didn't even chew their food. They ripped leaves off plants with their peg-shaped teeth and swallowed them whole. To help break up food in their stomachs, some dinosaurs would swallow stones!

Teeth of a carnivore

Teeth of a herbivore

Did You Know?

Dinosaurs could replace their teeth. One particular plant-eating dinosaur — *Diplodocus* — could grow replacement teeth in just 35 days.

Stomach Contents

Sometimes paleontologists are lucky enough to find fossilized bones of other animals inside a dinosaur's stomach. These extremely rare finds show what a dinosaur ate before it died.

Fossilized Feces

Another great way to learn about dinosaurs' diets is to look at fossilized feces. The scientific term for fossilized feces is coprolite. Bone, teeth, fur, plant stems, seeds, insects, fish scales, and shells have all been found in coprolites.

Mesozoic Salad Bar

The Mesozoic Era saw a huge increase in the diversity of plants on land. During this era, plants began to look like the plants of today. Ferns and palmlike plants dominated the early Mesozoic Era. Coniferous plants related to modern pines, cedars, and spruces soon emerged. By the late Mesozoic Era, flowering plants appeared. Flowering plants continue to thrive today.

Sago palms, more closely related to pines than palms, look similar to Mesozoic Era plants.

BECOME A FOSSIL HUNTER

Do you want to find a fossil? You might think fossils are extremely hard to find. This is true if you are set on finding a specific kind of fossil. But if you want to experience finding a fossil — any fossil — it's actually quite easy. In the United States and in other parts of the world, there are designated areas where fossil hunters are welcome. It's easy to find fossil-hunting sites near you. Ask an adult to help you search online for sites near your hometown.

Many museums and parks organize fossil-hunting events for kids. If you go on a fossil hunt, don't forget to be prepared. Like real paleontologists in the field, you will need to wear hiking boots and bring a notebook to record your findings. Remember that the fossil record is like an archive: it's an account of how life developed over a long time. If you find a fossil, take a moment to appreciate that you are holding a piece of ancient history in your hands.

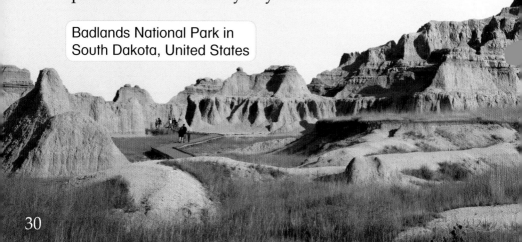

Badlands National Park in
South Dakota, United States

Accidental Discovery

In 2010 seven-year-old Kylie Ferguson was on vacation with her family in Badlands National Park, South Dakota. While participating in the National Park Service's Junior Ranger activities, Kylie came across a fossil. Kylie reported her find right away.

After rain had washed away some more soil around the fossil, paleontologists realized that Kylie's find was special. It turned out that Kylie had found a skull of an extinct saber-toothed cat — a rare find. The park's paleontologist praised Kylie for quickly reporting this discovery.

Kylie Ferguson poses with the fossilized cat skull that she discovered.

This is a reconstruction of a saber-toothed cat from the Natural History Museum in London, England.

Glossary

adapted: changed in order to be useful for a new task

adhesive: a substance with the ability to glue things together

analyzed: studied in detail in order to learn about an object

concentrations: numbers of things in a specific area

created: made

method: a process followed in order to successfully do something

preserved: kept intact or in good condition

radioactive: having or releasing radiation, a form of energy

reconstructions: things rebuilt to look like the originals

sediment: matter that sinks to the bottom and settles

specimens: objects that are collected and used as examples

transport: move from one place to another

Index